With big thanks to my wife Debbie
for technical support, and so much more besides.

Rough and Rowdy Days*

Odes to rock and roll

ALAN BUDGE

*With apologies to Bob Dylan
for riffing on his fine title

CONTENTS

MANIA

It started with She Loves You
On a northern market floor
One clan's life-long love affair
With the fabbest-ever four

We were buying Christmas records
The Bachelors, and Cliff
Dad made a face and muttered
'I suppose we must have *this*'

We took it home and played it
Howled those yeah yeah yeahs
Mum listened on, bewildered
As they went up through the gears

From then on, like some firestorm
Those songs kept pouring out
That conveyor belt of magic
No false turns, no doubts

Even mum liked All My Loving
And PS I Love You
Laughed as her little Beatles
Slaughtered Love Me Do

And they were just the moptops
A four-headed joy machine
John Paul George and Ringo
Singing for the Queen

And we were just the chorus
Countless millions strong
Safe within the knowledge
That they could do no wrong

Those first three years were something
An explosion of the soul
Four God-kissed scouser scallys
Reigniting rock and roll.

PLEASED TO MEET YOU

The trains head up to Charing Cross
Always have, and always will
Back in the fall of '61
A skinny boy waits, silent, still

Before the mystery train pulls in
He picks a bench, all lips, all grin
Plants his scrawny unknown butt
Down flat, and lights a cigarette
His hands wrapped fast around
Those priceless sleeves of US sound

Opposite, a guy,
All of seventeen
His legs, like uncoiled paperclips
Wind down to the ground

He carries a guitar.

They speak, (of course they speak)
'Hey now, what you got?'
'Berry, Muddy Waters, blues'
'I know what *that's* about'.

The train pulls into Charing Cross
The Rolling Stones step out.

SOUL MAN

'Who's song we gonna ruin today?'

The big man would ask with a smile
And the band locked right in
Brass, drums and guitar,
'Satisfaction' and 'My Girl' on trial

And *there,* all the while
A voice to crack wide
The tear ducts of stones
A rhythm so pure, undefiled

And when he sang live
The place came alive...

Dylan came down there one night
They met up backstage
'Now here's a new thing,
Fresh off the page
I've a feeling you'd do it just right'

So Bobby, he sang, and Otis he laughed
And 'Just Like a Woman' sat fine
'Oh yeah, I'll do that' the big man replied
Bob nodded, 'The pleasure's all mine'

***

And the plane took him up
And the plane took him down
And he never was given the time
To ruin Bob's song
Our loss all along
A soul sent to touch the divine.

INTO A TRANCE

I travelled west, to Belfast
My first visit there
Drifted down to Sandy Row
To take the morning air

The place meant something to me
Name-checked in a song
Laid down fifty years ago
(Say goodbye, so long)

Those afternoons I'd lay there
In that student room
Those love-lost days, those astral weeks
Atomised so soon

Oh yeah, we had the hard stuff
Our Zeppelin, our Doors
Then afternoons, the come-downs
Laid out on the floor

As words were spun on silk strings
A universe of sound
One song, *beyond* all others
Round and round and round

From hit-maker to heartache
From the USA, back home
To Belfast streets, to hail and sleet
To wander out alone

To make a kind of magic
Out of hunger, out of heat
Of something new-born, moving
Upon those city streets

Madame George, he called her
Translucent, ever new
You can glimpse her in the twilight
Down on Cyprus Avenue.

BLONDE ON BLONDE ON BLONDE

At eighteen, it's all to come
A last weekend at home
Before the earth began
To dip and spin on courses new...

And that last Friday night
I met a girl, she took me home
We sat and talked, and fooled around
She played me *Blonde on Blonde*

Between the tracks, between the sides
(And sometimes, the betweens were *long...*)
A clock ticked down the phantom hours
Three, three fifteen, four

As *Sad–eyed Lady* played again
All woozy grooves, all drifting moves
To the corners of the floor

'Let's have side two'
I Want You
On, and on some more.

I left at six, the autumn dawn
Rapping at my door
Whispering, 'This life, this time,
It's yours, it's yours, it's yours'

****

One week later, in the centre
Of my new home town
I called in at a record store
(Now isn't that what grants are for?)
And picked up *Blonde on Blonde*

And played it till it ached
Right through and into me

The voice, that wasted barbed-wire howl
Wrapped this one time in cotton wool
Those melodies, so clear, so clean
And the chaos of the world *exposed*
Insanities at play

Somehow this kid from nowhere
Had come across these shrouded paths
To the belly of the beast itself...
The shadow of our progress
The *price* of this success

He came back out and showed us
In words so stretched, so strange
Holding up a mirror
To the land of the deranged

And when he won that big prize
Thoughts turned to *Blonde on Blonde*
To love, inside the darkness
To sins left unatoned.

And, through the lives we've lived since
The fears, the joys, the tolls
These visions still reel me back in
These X-rays to the soul.

ALL YOU NEED

Picture yourself in the middle of something
Exploding in colours across the whole world
And somehow you manage to parcel the magic
For wide-eyed young boys and young girls

Ministers watching in jaw-dropping dread
How can this be, it's unreal
Reach for a sliver of some solid ground – and it's
gone...

Never to return, my friends, never to return
The kaleidoscope had shifted once, and shifted once
again
In '66, as hair and collars made the journey down
The Beatles put their feet up
To conjure sounds unbound

And all the kids came out to play
Those swinging London popinjays
Davies, Winwood, Barrett too
Light years away from Love Me Do

And through that giddy prism
Where anything's allowed
Permission had been given
To sing out, long and loud

And *were* we onto something
Through those hazy crazy days
Something touchable – untarnished
By the world and all its ways?

And oh, the precious pleasure
Of watching sureness fail
As the faces of our elders
Turned a whiter shade of pale.

GENERATION

The house lights down
The hall a winking, waiting space
We looked upon the stage
A mere arm-twirl away

I'd queued up overnight
For *these,* these tickets close on by
Seats down at the front
(We'd torn down fences, hoardings, signs
Towards that autumn dawn
The fire had burned so brightly
Its adverts kept us warm)

And *here* we were, expectant
Three thousand souls alight
With something rare, unfathomed
A burst of sheer delight

As out they stepped, the spotlights
Threw their shadows to the night
And *then* the place exploded
Six chords, and we were gone
Can't explain the feeling
As taut, unbroken voltage
Turned the whole place on

Through pop, hard rock, and 'opera'
Youth's acrid pulse defined
They brought it *all* on stage that night
Nothing left behind

Fire, water, earth and air
When elements collide
In fractious, fissile alchemy
Well, hold on for the ride

***

His mic, a flying arrow
Brought back down to scream
As if there's no tomorrow
Haunting all your dreams

The bass, a quartet on its own
Thunder in the dark
The man a still colossus
Never off the mark

The drummer incandescent
A swirling metronome
Of beat and freakish presence
'Excuse me, backing role?'

And Pete, his arm a-crashing down
On one more doomsday chord
When it came to firing up a stage...
Omega, the last word

Because, of all the runners
Those riders on the storm
Who came along to thrill us
On stages set, reborn

When they ask, who was it
Who stood out from the rest
Who were the greatest up there
I smile and say, 'Who's best.'

GOLD

The factories, all rusted now
The city pretty much shut down
One production line remains
Hard-wired into hearts and minds
In nightclubs, halls, fairgrounds

The sound of young America
A sassy, shining counterpoint
To all that rock and roll
Oh those heartbreak melodies
Beamed out of Detroit

And there I was, at fourteen
Eager for the whirl
Those ultra-violet dancehall lights
Flecking all with mystery
Who will be my girl?

Those handbags, in those circles
Those shy, delightful moves
The half-deciphered glances
Playing havoc with my senses
Stop, in the name of love

***

As Diana breathed of mountains
As Smokey shed his tears
The Temptations swirled the sound around
And Stevie sang, 'I'm yours'
I moved across the shadowed floor
A question in my eyes
She gave a half smile, took my hand
We headed for the exit sign
Found a quiet doorway
And kissed the time away
As Martha called across the night
We danced some, in the street

Now the songs remain, etched plain
On this old heart of mine
Sounds as sweet as spindrift silk
From the souls of street-wise lives
Upon this shoal of time

I hear the echoes down the years
The dreams, the longings, run aground
Yet what a joyous calling out
To laughter, loving, living proud
And farewell *is* a lonely sound.

THE WILD SIDE

I met Lou Reed once, shook his hand
He was as sweet as pie
Which only goes to show, I guess
The rumours sometimes lie

Clean and sober, happy, high
He'd just come off the stage
(I was there through friends of friends
Desperately unfazed)

I'd seen him, fifteen years before
At Charlton, back in '74
Peroxide blonde and wafer thin
A ghost presiding as the skin
Was ripped from rock and roll

He'd already done it all
A punk before the punks could crawl
Accomplice to the life of crime
The drugs part of the deal required
That vast, pernicious toll

'I hate all of those West Coast bands'
He'd said, in '68
As the Velvets cut a swathe between
The sinners and the saints

He told those stories as they came
The Janes, the femmes fatales
Between the skid row escapades
Waiting for his man

The hippies came, the hippies went
He waved them all goodbye
Smiled a smile as old as time
'Now, would I ever lie?'

And here he was, surviving
More than that, at peace
His heirs still multiplying
Granted sweet release

So yeah, there are these lodestones
These markers on the souls
Of boys and girls whose lives were saved
Saved by rock and roll.

OOOOOH YEAH

My younger sister brought it home
Borrowed from an older boy
Who'd said, 'You must hear this.'

I opened up the gatefold sleeve
To see an airship, bathed in gold
Four names upon the plinth...
Put it on the Dansette
Turned the volume high

And that was it for me.

Now, there are riffs, and bigger riffs
And then there's *this*
A calling card, a call to arms
As potent as the days were long
That summer, 1970

At fourteen, I was ripe for gods
And here they were -
Remote, unfathomed, free
Providers of the greatest joys
Diviners of those boundaries
Between what is...

And what should never be

Sometimes a visitation
Inside a concert hall
Those palaces of ecstasy
Whipping up a storm

We could reach
But never touch them
We could feel
But never know
The force that passed
Between them
In that occult glow

No Facebook posts, no Twitter feeds
No guest slots on the week's TV
No write-ups in the daily news
A few lines in the music press
Was all it ever took
Before the next LP

Their faces vanished, one by one
Between the third and fourth release
(And there the name went too)
We only had the music
Those heavy metal blues

Those drums like thunder on the plains
Always on the beat
Those bass and organ-filled delights
The voice a gentle murmured sigh
Gliding to those shrieking heights
Guitar as fluid as the night
Or quiet, softly spent...

They came, they saw, we said OK
Message understood
The thing about Led Zeppelin
They were really fucking good.

MARLEY'S GHOST

And as he left those Trenchtown streets
We never knew, or guessed
What this man would bring us
Looking upward, heading west

A smile like lightning, sounds like silk
A voice as pure as dread
Man he shook our souls apart
Wasn't nothing left unsaid

Say, I remember, seeing him
Guitar, and nothing... save
That voice, all spectral questioning
One last unlocked offering
Across the water, icy, skimmed
'All I ever have...'

He came, he told, he went on by
Ashes into dust
We're left to wonder at the sky
In I and I we trust.

THE LOWDOWN

Tucked away inside this stream
Of half-remembered, tinted dreams
We have our own pet sounds
Awarded private crowns

The ones adopted, taken in
At confidential gatherings
Our secret hidden gold
(Feel free to choose your own)

Our guy was Boz Scaggs

That lowdown groove
Those neon moves
So smoothly now, loves lost
Counting every cost

Inside the sweetest strings around
The cocksure bass, *that* trumpet sound
The voice a silk sigh to our ears
Spooling out those golden years...

The nights we stayed up past the dawn
Plucking magic from the air
Laughter falling everywhere
Then leaning back and drifting down
We'd listen to 'We're All Alone'
And steal a peace we'd never known.

THAT STUPID CLUB

His grave's a paltry place, at best
Squeezed between the other stones
North-east of Paris, Pere Lachaise
An afterthought, almost

Room here for one more inside
Killed off, like all the rest
By dreams, and drugs, and alcohol
The brightest and the best

Oh Jim could sing
The Doors could bring
A hefty dose of all things dark...
On all that hippy happenstance
They left their scabrous mark

And Jimi went, an accident
We play, and sometimes burn
He played like heaven sent him down
Then begged for his return

Brian never had a chance
All sex and talent, nothing more
Heading for that open door...

Janis, with her ball and chain
Addictions, built to last
All the stuff she took to fly
Catching up too fast

She left us with a palimpsest
Of lost souls torn apart
Of something, somewhere good enough
A piece of that bruised heart.

***

All gone, at twenty seven
Just like the morning rain
Off to join that stupid club
A mother's tired refrain.

COMPLEX FRAGILE PURE

Genesis. The Free Trade Hall.
1973
A row of boys (*all* boys of course)
Up in the gallery

We sat in silence, awed, enthralled
These guys knew how to play
Progressive rock, we called it
Tomorrow's 'Yesterday'

Oh man, I saw them all
Swaddled in my greatcoat
Focus, Tull, and E.L.P
(Sadly, only P remains)
We'd listen hard there, after school
To beats unbound
To Mesolithic proto-sounds
Our conversations, round and round
Just who can play the best?
 - or fastest anyway
Guitarists ranked by God knows what
(None of us could play a chord)
Keyboard players eulogised
Rick Wakeman, Wright, Jon Lord.

***

Three years on, the Pistols came
And 'played' a side venue
The Lesser Free Trade Hall
And all those prog guys packed their bags
And rode out of our minds
Left not a trace behind

(And yes, there was a *lot* of crap
Topographic ocean-wide
The stables were indeed in need
Of dinosauricide...)

But, you know, four years before
Back in '72
I'd been there at the Free Trade Hall
When Pink Floyd had unveiled a thing
Called Dark Side of the Moon
A year before the record hit
We heard it first, as fresh as paint
As spookily deranged as saints
On acid could arrange

And it blew our tiny minds

And today, my son enjoys
'And You and I', for sure
I like a bit of Yes myself
Complex, fragile, pure.

NO FUTURE

I have in my possession
A ticket to a gig
It cost almost two quid
(It was a while ago)

As a tail-end hippy
I'd bathed in all the trippy
Early 70s stuff: *E.L.P* and *Jethro Tull*
And yes, well, *Yes* of course

And we hadn't seen it coming
This bolt out of the blue
The NME, our seismograph
Our bringer of the new

The tremors were detected
Around late '76.
Not so much a new sound
As a kick against the pricks

So we went down to the Roxy
To check out all the fuss
Rank and dank and nasty
As befits *this* business

And then the Queen got old enough
To celebrate something
While, somewhere in North London
A non-idea took wing

The Pistols had already
Carved a bloody trail
Through the tortured heads of wayward boys
Looking to swerve jail

I bought the single early June
Played nothing else for days
God Save the Queen, as England's dream
Vanished in the haze

Soon, you see, as collars shrank
As jeans became unflared
We took to wearing blacks and blues
And meat-cleavered our hair

We caught the Damned, and Blondie
Watched Television play
The Jam, the Blockheads, 'Elvis'...
The Clash blew them all away

Strummer in his element
Centre stage, bereft
Of any hint of compromise
What else was there left?

So we queued up for our tickets
The week before the show
Down in St Pauls, the beating heart
Of Bristol's ganga glow

The Pistols at the Bamboo Club
A week to wait, that's all
Around day three, the club burned down
Someone missed the call.

We still went out that Wednesday night
We scoured the streets of Bristol
On the lookout for stray Pistols...

Nowhere to be seen
There was no information
I had no information
Just that piece of card.

They burst apart a few weeks on
The comet flared and died
They'd lit the fuse, paid all their dues
Nowhere left to hide.

.

NOW AND THEN

And so began those four decades'
Diminishing returns
All those rock messiahs
Was nothing ever learned?

Oh, we had our pop stars
Our Culture Club, our Prince
But much, too much
Has slipped away
That desire for something more
Than all this mute decay

(Or is this special pleading
A boomer's sourest grapes?
A sense of lifetimes closing in
No more great escapes?)

And yet, there *were* those fetters
A generation tied
Against their will, we hear it still
In the music, in those cries
A sense that there was more at stake
A culture gone world-wide
More to win and lose, my friends
Revolution - from inside

Besides, the music's what it is
A renaissance of the heart
The words, the melodies remain
Ragamuffin works of art.

ONLY ROCK AND ROLL?

I took my son to see the Stones
A year or so ago
My boy, at ten, a captive fan
All his sweet short life
I'd driven him around
To those wasted, weighted sounds…

And here now, here we are.

The thing you see is this
I'd seen them first at Earls Court
Over forty years ago
Past it *then,* the common view
How can lifetimes *disappear*
And this lot still be here?

I'd imagined sitting, not quite still
A polite foot tapping, now and then
An evening to reflect
On all the ways a life can move
Between that teenage promise
And the stuff we all go through

My son, all quiet, waiting
Examining the stage
Until the scrawny beasts emerged
Plugged in, began to play

And when they hit those first chords
'Street Fighting Man' rang clear
Startling, stirring, unabashed…

And I vanished down the years

There I was, a fan again
Reclaimed, re-tuned, alive
To the purest dose of rock and roll
This side of paradise

***

And, after Keith had sung his bit
Halfway through the show
The sky grown dark
The stage lights down
A mist of dry ice swirling round
The ghostliest 'whoo whoos'

The boy there, sitting next to me
Glanced across and grinned
The recognition plain
'Now I wonder what *this* is'
I murmured
Happy as a man can be
As the singer took the stage

'Please allow me to introduce myself'
The sly old rogue growled out
As chords the size of Rushmore
Spun the night about

***

And then that giddy slalom
Through the greatest greatest hits
And down there, in 'Brown Sugar'
The singer walked across
Waved his arms to draw the shouts
Ten thousand yeah yeah yeahs

And I caught a glimpse of someone else
A kid who didn't care
What anybody thought about
His looks, his lips, his hair
And I felt a surge of something
You might call it gratitude
For all those guys had given us…

Because they loved the blues

And here, tonight, these decades on
A message from the music's core
At seventeen or seventy
Something vital, primal, pure
Comes on down the line

How were the Stones?
Just fine.

ROUGH AND ROWDY DAYS

And how many roads have we all walked down
Since the kid from Hibbing wrote the sounds
That lit a match inside a world
Dying to be born?

He gave us something *other*
A way of testing faith
In fathers, sisters, brothers
Are you going to play it safe?

He took us disappearing
Down those echo-shadowed lanes
Those vacant lots of memory
We wandered down alone
To wait beneath the sign that read
There's no direction home.

He didn't save our lives, our souls
Nothing to redeem
But aah, the joy of *knowing*
Life isn't what it seems

***

And then, at eighty, more or less
He came to say once more
Some things that needed saying
A knock on Heaven's door

And there he sits so patiently
The cards still in his hands
Telling how things might have been
And the lies of this new land

And we listen, close, as ever
As he conjures time away
Now, and then, *forever*
Those rough and rowdy days.

SOMETHING TO BE

There was a lucky man
Who made the grade
'One two three four, boys
We got it made'

There was a man who charmed
Sounds from the sky
With words to make us sigh
And laugh, and cry

There was a time it seemed
He had it all
We fell down on our knees
And hit free fall

(We raise them up on high
We cast them down
Want blessings from some guy
Beneath some crown)

There was an angry man
Who found some peace
He walked into the dark
And nailed the beast

There was a man who smiled
Signed autographs
Four thousand million miles
From one last laugh

There was a man who died
Was here, then gone
A star torn from the sky...
Whose light shines on.
.

SACRED NOISE
-   (10TH JANUARY 2016)

There is a roadhouse in the sky
Just this side of Paradise
Where the stars come out to play

A pair of Scouser scallywags
The weathered, leathered West Coast star
That cool cat from New York
And the guy who *was* guitar

Two drummer boys still three parts mad
Laying down the pace
And, to one side, as cool as fuck
A man in black, on bass

The lights go down, the band strikes up
Loose *and* tight, and quite unlike
Anything on Earth
The audience, those waifs and strays
The ones whose lives were rearranged
By all this sacred noise
Stare at the waiting mike
Lit by one spotlight...

A cold wind blows, the door swings back
A man there, in a snap-brimmed hat
'Hey David – come inside'.

***

(And out below the starlight
Beneath a sleepy moon
A sign hangs by the roadside
'The Beatles: coming soon.')

As one by one they leave the stage
We say goodbye, adieu
We'll never see their like again
As the man said, 'Uh huh huh.'

ABOUT THE AUTHOR

Alan Budge grew up with the Beatles, and grew his hair to Led Zeppelin. He has worked in everything from would-be smart London restaurants to ground-breaking charitable organisations. He lives in the Peak District, and now divides his time between writing, walking and discussing Dylan lyrics with a close-knit group of like-minded lunatics.